Understanding the Forbidden

"Understanding/graphic essay"
www.maxmilo.com
ISBN : 978-2-31501-368-5

Henri-Pierre Jeudy
Aleksi Cavaillez

Understanding the Forbidden

1. The Mania for Prohibition

JACQUES DUTRONC'S FAMOUS SONG "FAIS PAS CI, FAIS PAS ÇA, VIENS ICI, METS-TOI LÀ" REVEALS THE EXTENT TO WHICH CHILDREN LIVE IN AN ENVIRONMENT PUNCTUATED BY A PROLIFERATION OF PROHIBITIONS. Any initiative on his part seems to be nullified, as if the impossibility of living his freedom were his primary condition. The song ends like this: "Don't worry guys, I've been told that too, and it's come to this." The humor of such a ritornello marries the repetitive, infernal cadence of the prohibition, and offers a salvific ending that suggests that the harassment of prohibitions in no way prevents the possibility of living. It's a similar philosophical turnaround that children can make when they realize that "everything is possible" precisely because everything is forbidden. **How else can we experience the possible than by opposing prohibition?**

The child's irreducible joy in doing what is forbidden comes from the countless ways in which he opposes the prohibition. More often than not, he relies on the exhausting effect of repeating the negative injunction from the adult, who would eventually scratch his voice by shouting so loudly. He can also "do everything" on the sly, until he's caught in the act of breaking the rules. But the idea that the world can belong to him presupposes a permanent play with the "atmosphere of proscription" stimulated by prohibitions. The more we tell him not to do this or that, the more he'll do it, and this infantile mania, which sometimes lasts well into old age, presents itself as the break-in of desire. Our spirit of rebellion, which does not disappear over time, comes up against the excesses of complacency that we maintain with moral comfort. **The temptation to say the wrong thing or do the wrong thing haunts us, because it coincides with the extent to which we exercise our freedom.**

As a child, the first prohibition that fascinated me was the inscription on the bottom of railroad carriage windows: "Il est dangereux de se pencher au dehors" ("It's dangerous to lean out"). Rolling down the window and sticking your head out must have been a common temptation. You can see the landscape pass by behind the glass, and yet you're tempted to put your head in to enter the picture. It's not the same as lifting or drawing a curtain, behind which, a Lacanian psychoanalyst would tell you, you'll discover nothing. Nor is it the Kantian's impossible passage from phenomenon to noumenon, or the Platonic experience of the myth of the cave… It's just a matter of plunging your head into the wind of an inaccessible reality, because the traces of black dust on the glass veil the landscape, especially when it starts to rain, or for the good reason that a train could come up in the opposite direction and decapitate you. Was that advice rather than a prohibition? I knew, as all children do, that there are things not to see or do. But was it dangerous? This presentiment of what is prohibited, without knowing the meaning of the word *prohibition*, put me in the common state, to say the least, of wanting to see what I shouldn't see. But it was much later, when I had grown up, that the young boy in me understood that he shouldn't look too closely at his mother's or his sister's sex.

This relationship between the invocation of danger expressed by "it's dangerous to lean outside" and the prohibition of incest is not self-evident, unless we admit that, in the child's imagination, the outside is the sex of the other, the one he must not see. Today, such a scene can no longer occur, since air-conditioned carriages have irremovable windows. The landscape remains forever on the other side of the glass, and "sticking your head out" while on the train is no longer a temptation.

FROM NOW ON, CHILDREN CAN USE PROHIBITIONS AGAINST ADULTS, including their own parents who commit a health-threatening offence in their presence. "You want us dead!"

they exclaim when their father lights a cigarette in the car. This use of prohibitions enables children themselves to control their parents' actions, reminding them, not without irony, that their "good behavior" should serve as an example. Advertising uses the child as an active prescriber, imposing both driving and health standards. **Children are no longer**

simply subjected to prohibitions; they have the power to "call to order" their own parents when they fail to apply the standards required to protect their lives.

In an order governed by standards for survival, the challenge is to learn to "forbid" anything that threatens life, considering that it's a matter of applying obligations that have become "natural". This is why blatant rejection of a ban—such as smoking—is seen as a sign of infantile regression. Doing the wrong thing is a sign of irresponsibility. The prohibitions that govern everyday life also seem to respond to vital necessities for the future of humanity. Sanitary, prophylactic and environmental reasons always legitimize norms. What is the relationship between the forbidden and the norm?

THE NORMATIVE SPACE IN WHICH WE LIVE, WHETHER PRIVATE OR PUBLIC, CANNOT BECOME EFFICIENT IF IT IS NOT SUPPORTED BY A COMMON WILL TO PROHIBIT. Recognition of what is harmful to health forges the unmistakable objectivity of the norm. In this way, the meaning given to the ban itself would not be called into question, since it would have a universal ecological quality. **This legitimacy of standards becomes a moral foundation for the ban. In a way, it's the common good that must be preserved.** How can we doubt a ban that is imposed in the name of reason and the

good of all? It's no longer a person who dictates prohibitions, it's the prohibition itself that publicly displays its validity. No longer will anyone need to say: "Thou shalt not do that", the ban will automatically personalize itself in each of our gestures (or eco-gestures). Its role is to no longer appear itself as a prohibitive sign, thanks to the incredible effect of its imposition as an absolute necessity. "I don't do this or that because it's forbidden, but because it's vital and necessary. So I give myself the illusion that I'm doing it of my own free will. Sharing a didactic approach to everyday life, based on understanding and applying norms, seems to help us imagine a possible future life.

YET SUCH A SHARED RECOGNITION OF USEFULNESS SEEMS TO BE CONTRADICTED BY INDIVIDUAL OR COMMUNITY ANGER. Il est interdit d'interdire" ("It is forbidden to forbid"), the provocative injunction of May 68, has become a slogan whose power of suggestion remains anachronistic but still relevant today. It may seem naïve and outdated, because it invokes an ideal of absolute freedom that is proving impossible, but it endures as the horizon of revolts against all abuses of authority. Of course, not all prohibitions come from the exercise of power, and when they become norms whose necessity seems inescapable, their role is no longer to deny "our" freedom, but to protect it. **In the space of a few decades, the rise of ecology has revealed the extent to which the choice and imposition of norms to "save the planet" has become a primordial requirement.** As a result, prohibition seems to have turned on its head as a guarantee of collective survival. Protecting every chance of saving "our" freedom presupposes the "natural" respect of prohibitions, without these being experienced as such. Does this paradoxical reversal change the way we imagine "our" freedom? The incentive to eco-responsibility is the prospect of a future built on the collective recognition of a shared, objective rationality that would cancel out the very representation of the forbidden.

If, in 1968, the prohibition decried was of a moral nature, even before being parental, the teenager's revolt is expressed against what he sees as an abuse of power. When a teacher handing out homework is called a "Nazi", it's fair to ask whether questioning his or her power is inappropriate. All the most devious means are good enough to satisfy the adolescent who poses as a subject denouncing authoritarianism. The duty curiously becomes the representation of the forbidden against which he rebels, and authority would in this sense be the expression of the prohibition against not doing "one's" homework. **The forbidden is presented as a reversible figure: it contains what must be done and what must not be done, but what must be done is always deduced from what must not be done.**

If the prohibition is objective, it is no longer represented by a person, and it is the injunction to respect it that reintroduces the presence of an authority. On a bus, should the driver intervene to call to order a passenger who passes in front of him without a ticket? If he doesn't, is he complicit in the fraud? If it's forbidden to travel without a ticket, the agent is responsible for ensuring that the rule is respected. On Paris buses, a new inscription has been affixed to the middle window: "Si chacun fait ses règles, tout se dérègle". It proves that the call to civility is more essential than the injunction of prohibitions. If someone says to you: "You're taking the space reserved for the stroller" in a tone of voice that's not at all friendly, they're signalling a breach of the rule by telling you to move over, even though you're not in a position to comply because there are too many people. Strollers are imposed like little tanks that must be circumvented at the cost of incredible contortions to consecrate the place of the child in a society where demography was in peril. I can't say loud and clear: "It's forbidden to step on my toes! Are civil relationships becoming exchanges of summonses?

Everyone has noticed that the smoking ban has created a new atmosphere in public spaces. On café terraces, in the spring sunshine, smokers and non-smokers are forced to rub shoulders. Non-smokers hope that one day smoking will be banned in all public spaces, as they are forced to share with smokers the enjoyment of the arbitrariness of a law they would have liked even more radical. **Nevertheless, smokers seem to play with the rules like children.** In the courtyard of the famous Chartier restaurant in Paris, several pictograms indicate that smoking is forbidden there. I saw an Asian woman with a cigarette on her lips send her smoke against the famous symbol. I approached her to ask why she was taking this posture, and she said, "It's what gives me the most pleasure." She was blowing smoke in the face of the forbidden. Curiously, the slightest transgression is considered an ostentatious gesture in the public space. Some men "relieve themselves" despite the presence of a sign forbidding urination, consisting of several lines that are impossible for them to read when they feel the urge. Is the ban there to contain the satisfaction of an urge that hardly seems able to wait? And what can women do?

Each of us harbors a desire for a forbidden situation that we'd like to impose on others. On public transport, this desire becomes very active. It first crystallizes on the smell of the other person. How can we publicly forbid "smelling bad"? No one can ignore the fact that the attraction or repulsion that stimulates the sense of smell remains cultural. In some countries, we hear that the French don't wash. There are people who sweat, and there are those who believe they are lucky enough to be odorless. Promiscuity exacerbates the violence of repulsion when we feel our vital space is threatened. The place a body occupies, and the way it produces an unbearable odor, can provoke disgust. Given the variety of odoriferous signs, imagine the number of pictograms that would be needed if the prohibitions desired by people who grumble on public transport were drawn on the windows. The imagination of the forbidden addressed to the other in raging silence knows no measure. If tolerance is not the result of choice, is it exercised as an agreed obligation to keep up appearances?

WE SHOULD ASK OURSELVES HOW THE SPREAD OF THE DESIRE TO FORBID (ALWAYS FOR THE OTHER AND NOT FOR ONESELF) CAN BECOME A DISEASE OF THE SOCIAL BODY. The consensualism produced by the multiplication of prohibitions turns against any ostensible gesture of transgression, whether unintentional or not, which is struck down as reckless or in bad faith. With regard to ecological norms, we are thus invited to note the extent to which prohibition, understood and accepted for its universal necessity, is the very sign of the shared intelligence of a society that finds itself capable of reflecting on its destiny instead of consenting to catastrophe. **Can the atmosphere of prohibition be amplified without the risk of becoming too heavy, without engendering too much suspicion, as a benefit for the future of humanity?** Any ban imposed for ecological reasons makes the attempt to transgress it grotesque. I can be annoyed by prohibitions, but not by norms that I have to accept as "well-founded". The norm has an aura, so to speak, that gives the ban its raison d'être. So rebelling against prohibitions seems childish when they display the power of the environmental norm. I can sometimes laugh at the complexity of waste sorting, but I can no longer make fun of the principle itself without appearing ridiculous and inconsistent. When constraint provokes an automatic reaction that makes us forget its power, it gains in trivialization what it loses in coercive effect. In this way, everyone ends up obeying environmental standards without even thinking about it.

Faced with the development of a normative rationality accomplished in the name of human survival, behavior considered deviant is stamped with the seal of infantile regression. **As a measure, the forbidden becomes the raison d'être of a balanced life.** The greater its normative power, the greater society's capacity for reflexivity, enabling it to secure its future. Recognition of the forbidden is the tangible sign of responsibility. Those who fail to respect the legitimacy of the proscription are irresponsible. Normativity, creating a form of social atmosphere in everyday life, is based on the indissoluble link between prescription and proscription: what is prescribed takes on meaning and finality with what is proscribed.

But such is the paradox: the more we are forced to feel responsible, the more we are besieged by the nagging impression of powerlessness. We hear that people no longer react, that they are resigned to accepting whatever measures are taken to ward off their anxieties about the future. In this way, a collective feeling of powerlessness takes refuge behind the observation of a "state of affairs" against which nothing can be done. It also seems to find an alternative in a consensual, universal humanitarianism that makes any depiction of a loss of our freedoms unseemly. As horrors and misfortunes are broadcast by the media, the collective exercise of commiseration gives *a sacrificial meaning to restriction.* All the guilt that may arise from the daily vision of misery and distress is transferred to the organization of massive compassion towards those who claim a "right to". The claim to a "right to", whatever its object, reveals the extent to which the aspiration to be able to survive calls for humanist indulgence. Until recently, when we spoke of the welfare state, the individual positioned himself "as a victim" to claim the aid necessary for survival. Today, he is both "victim" and "responsible", which in short defines his powerlessness. This allows political power to display the appearance of its real and immediate effectiveness in any situation, by staging its ability to intervene. The simulation of what resembles the state of exception that characterizes totalitarianism legitimizes all possible restrictions.

The way out of a crisis, whether economic, ecological or for other reasons, is to make a shared sacrifice. More than ever, we need to learn to "forbid ourselves"! This spirit of parsimony is more mental than economic, since consumption is actually doing quite well. "Forbidding ourselves" from overspending means recognizing a necessity that dispenses with freedom of choice.

A few years ago, an advertising video for the Audi car brand began by showing a man who went berserk when he discovered his freedom. We see him taking off his clothes

one after the other, throwing them in the air, in a state of exaltation, as if he were freeing himself from all constraints. When he's almost naked, he watches an Audi car go by. Gradually, he puts his clothes back on and regains his middle-management look, complete with suit, tie and briefcase. The moral of the story appears with this question: "Do we have the freedom to choose?" Freedom of choice was the driving force behind consumption, and all advertising worked by encouraging consumers to live in the expectation of longing for what they wanted. This advertising sequence shows, on the contrary, that consumption is a collective obligation. There's no longer any need to exalt the desire to buy; the logic of consumption is imposed as the sole purpose of life. We can choose mechanically between one product and another, but the feeling of being free to choose must first disappear behind the truism of necessity.

Choice is legitimized by "I have no choice". Whether it's a political election or an ecological, cultural or social program, the same observation applies: the prior freedom to choose is an obstacle that must be overcome by accepting the reality of the need to consume.

It is always in the name of the economic crisis, the disarray it provokes, the fear of social, health or other disasters, that the correctness of the decisions adopted remains indisputable. Taken as a rule, the obvious becomes an absolute necessity. "We can't do otherwise, it's common sense! Changing social behavior is no longer a dream, but the expected effect of collective restrictions made objectively necessary, even though they allow some to grow richer while others grow poorer. Resistance is then seen as the harmful consequences of an organization that has seen the end of the great social conquests. **Isn't living with the times a rational and parsimonious anticipation of life?**

There is growing suspicion of those who fail to comply with norms, and the call for different lifestyles, which should correspond to new approaches to "living together", results above all in an increasingly obsessive organization of control. Coercive models of the "new hope" offered by everyday energy saving are legitimized by the assignment to live "differently". We can denounce those who don't sort their garbage properly, or those who let their water run excessively, but why not those who take photographs of the earth from their plane? Without indulging in the rather contradictory habits of rational parsimony for the good of all, it is perhaps preferable to consider that the worst could happen if nothing is done to control the risks of disaster when we are sure that humanity and planet Earth are running together to their doom. It is this kind of ideological framing, which is increasingly universal, that consecrates the contemporary atmosphere of coercion and the apotheosis of a rationality of our freedom.

2. The Reign of Survival

THE PUBLIC HEALTH ECONOMY JUSTIFIES INCREASINGLY COERCIVE CONTROL OF PRIVATE LIFE, and the body belongs less and less to each individual, who is obliged to consider it as a commodity whose instructions work to his or her detriment. Dietary advice, for example, is immediately seen as forbidden, because it is the only objective condition for ensuring a shared future. And public health measures carry this future forward as the triumph of a humanity capable of protecting itself against the risks of its decline. What used to be debatable is no longer so: the breakdown of our society is due to excessive tolerance of those who threaten our collective survival. **Accepting prohibitions, segregation by control, is in a way protecting us from ourselves, from the tendencies we have to abuse everything that destroys us.** The spread of smoking bans in public spaces is a fundamental test of how far a community can resign itself to accepting the rules imposed for its survival. Any prophylactic treatment of pollution sets an example. Its implementation is a means of gauging predisposition to collective resignation. In a social atmosphere where everyone can be stigmatized as a polluter, public authorities have every right to exercise their sovereignty by taking measures that guarantee the salvation of the community.

A society's equilibrium depends on its members' ability to recognize the senselessness of their revolt and indignation. In the name of the majority, resignation to new forms of subjugation, legitimized by the imperatives of institutional and individual survival, would be the only possible collective behavior for the future of a liberal democracy. Such resignation renders unnoticeable the figures of coercion that the power of accepted constraints produces.

We all remember the controversy caused by the photograph of a supermodel with an anorexic body. Was it simply intended to show the horror behind fashion's staging? The young woman's emaciated body was taken to symbolize the tyranny of an "aesthetic of thinness". As long as the emaciated body is presented at a fashion show, it is of no concern to anyone; its excessive thinness remains trivialized, so to speak. The same body has to be isolated and shown as the disastrous effect of aesthetic imperatives on the "model" for the general commotion to occur. When the public image of horror is created, the horror itself is no more than the expected effect of a victimization that feeds collective compassion. Yet, symbolically, the body of the young anorexic woman shows that she has no choice, that she is obliged to the point of excess to practice the restrictions necessary to remain a supermodel. What she reveals is that the absence of choice, absolute submission to standards of any kind, leads to a slow death. *Necessity is the law*, as the saying goes. **But if necessity takes the place of the law and gives it its meaning, there's nothing left to do but surrender to the evidence of constraints.**

When a doctor prescribes remedies for his patient, he usually accompanies his written prescription with prohibitions that he first enunciates orally. First and foremost, alcohol and tobacco are forbidden, as they may neutralize the therapeutic effects expected from the use of medication. The incompatibility between the supposed benefits of wine and the ingredients that regulate our body is the source of the ban. Insofar as we recognize that it is for our own good, it is the prohibition that can save us from ourselves and from our tendencies to create a certain imbalance. **Since it seems almost natural for everyone to seek the right balance, prohibition is clearly necessary for indivi-**

dual and collective survival, since it is the weapon that prevents excess. Without it, no balance would be possible. This morning, I won't drink a glass of mirabelle plum, as I've always done, because it's my only chance of not dying prematurely. I reassure myself that I'm the one doing the forbidding, but is it true? Instead, I'm adopting a collective norm that applies to the set of rules that govern the eventual increase in longevity. And if I say to myself: "I've got to die some time", I give the sad impression of an existential resignation. Is it the recognition of the risk of dying that dictates my conduct? Or am I subject to the imperative that it is now forbidden to die?

Smoke less, drink less, eat less fat… The need for a certain parsimony seems to give meaning to life every day, and the primary reason for the countless daily norms is to maintain the body's equilibrium, achieved through the obligatory enjoyment of restrictions. Whether psychic, organic, financial or other, the economy legitimizes the forbidden by offering it the figure of a vital requirement. The political advantage of the economy in everyday life is to occupy people's minds, making them believe that only the intelligence of consumption counts. And this staging of a strange delirium of intelligibility should make us realize that any new norm is the fruit of in-depth collective reflection on

its necessity. **This would be society's most conventional paradox: there are never any senseless standards.** Norms can be misapplied, they can fail, and the arbitrariness that constitutes them is only betrayed by the whining of the recalcitrant or the obsessed with legal procedure. The

ban is no longer merely moral; it has become ecumenical. Its universality seems self-evident.

WHEN WE LOOK AT OUR OWN BODY IN THE MIRROR, WE ACCEPT TO SEE WHAT IT'S BECOMING BECAUSE WE'RE CERTAIN THAT IT CAN'T BE OTHERWISE, even if the use of cosmetics or sporting practices offers us the possibility of imagining that we're delaying what it's becoming. We are confronted with what our body "should be" rather than what it is. This is the repeated scene of the invocation of prohibitions, because restrictions and prohibitions are seen as the best way to survive, the body's balance being achieved above all through deprivation. **The body's harmony and coherence are merely the result of daily submission to norms designed to ward off the temptation of excess. It's all part of an "integrated normativity" that obscures any reflection on the meaning and use we give to the forbidden.** The habits we adopt to care for and maintain our bodies no longer need to be thought through, and the built-in prohibition can be forgotten. In fact, it has even disappeared, as agreed obligations become signs of "my" freedom to maintain my body. Its shortcomings are no longer simply the result of an organic imbalance, but of "misbehavior" that distorts the validity of survival norms. All the representations we have of our body are finalized by what we deem "good" for it. This is why we naturalize the norms that govern what we imagine to be our body's ideal harmony. So we treat our own body as an object of preservation threatened by its ineluctable degradation. We also treat it with suspicion, since it is capable of betraying tendencies that could jeopardize it. We refuse to consider "what the body can do" (Spinoza). Unlike the "vitalists" of the late 19th century, we don't believe in the power of the life instinct, preferring to opt for contemporary models of survival, and refusing to recognize the body's capacity for self-regulation.

The body becomes an enemy, or perhaps even our worst enemy, since in the intoxication of its excesses, it never ceases to circumvent us. If we take up Nietzsche's idea that *the body makes no mistakes*, the prohibitions imposed on it to ensure its survival are no more than palliatives. Their application denies the possible exercise of its coherence through a "normative proliferation" that besieges us. Such is the example set by the regime's obsessives. The fight against addiction to anything that makes us obese is never more than a parry. The power of the norm in dieting does not take on the form of tyranny, because it comes from its implicit acceptance, made necessary beforehand. This *naturalization of norms* makes any transgression an illicit act.

Yet the pleasure of the illicit remains a temptation, at all times in everyday life, when it takes as its object limits to be circumvented. We could almost speak of a "culture of the illicit", particularly encouraged by a consumer society. Aren't these everyday games of transgression, of circumventing limits, always stimulated by a

spirit of vindication and revenge, forging, even if they are joyful, the contemporary figure of a certain miserablism of revolt? Impotence becomes a "revengeful" parody of a transgression that has no impact on the foundations of common rules. When we believe we can appeal to our free will, our denunciation of the arbitrariness of the norm consists in trying to make its legitimacy inescapable. If a driver says: "With my big engine, if I drive at a hundred and thirty kilometers an hour, I risk falling asleep, I'm becoming dangerous", he's denouncing a limit that he contests by saying that his level of vigilance rises with the increase in his vehicle's speed. He may be acting in good faith, but his reasoning is fallacious, even if he's not wrong. It's by making the arbitrary nature of the norm apparent that we believe we can display "our" free will.

Is the pleasure of the illicit condemned to the expression of its irrationality? From now on, it will be forbidden to "touch" the arbitrariness of a norm in the name of some freedom of estimation of what ought to be. It's a radical way of protecting any normative system. The "new forbidden" are all the more easily integrated into the public space as they are already part of a normative atmosphere. There's a certain nostalgia for the poetry of the rules on the walls of the bistros of yesteryear. In Brazil, in the *gafieras* where they dance the samba, there's always this injunction that makes you dream: it's forbidden to flirt. Dancing is dancing! These are the rules of the game. But nowadays, the prohibitions are piling up. The question then arises, in the public arena, as to whether a ban that hides another is just as likely to cancel out one of the previous ones, or one of the following ones. **Will we**

experience freedom through the confusion of contradictory prohibitions?

WHAT'S MOST FRIGHTENING IS THE ANTICIPATION OF THE PRODUCTION OF THE FORBIDDEN. There will never be enough of them! We now have the disconcerting impression that bans create atmosphere, just like in a nightclub. No doubt it's the cult of the forbidden that's spreading like wildfire to optimize the day-to-day management of otherness. It has to be said: it's always the other person who is forbidden, the one who doesn't respect it. This is what drives social relations: "What you're doing here will soon be forbidden! The margin of freedom left to us would therefore be destined to shrink over time, confirming the adage *I'm doing it while there's still time*. It's enough to believe that, if the human being is by nature a polluter, purification will be achieved by multiplying the number of prohibitions to finally live in a completely sanitized society. Long before I was born, in a state considered embryonic, I was undoubtedly polluted by my mother, who at the time smoked cigarillos with impunity during her pregnancy. In the old days, we simply said to each other: "It's not advisable. **Since human beings don't listen to advice, the forbidden will do its good in spite of itself.**

Does anticipation have a conjuring effect? That would be too good! Without needing to be stated, the prohibition could remain implicit, as a possible, desirable sign of prevention. "Take some precaution…". But no, the precautionary principle, contemporary war machine against the harmful effects of pollution of all kinds, anticipates for us. A cartoon depicted a driver in a traffic jam bending his head out of his car window to call a passer-by walking along the sidewalk smoking his cigar a polluter. The eternal question "Who are the polluters?" is repeated like a litany of impotence in the face of the most contradictory causes of pollution. **Is the ban simply a sign of the failure of objective rationality in prevention?**

We hear people say, "You shouldn't do this, you shouldn't do that, but everyone has their own freedom!" Are we free to do or not to do? Isn't this the sweet illusion of a freedom we imagine we have? I can also imagine that I set the ban myself. It's the decision to resist the temptation of evil, not necessarily in the name of moral rules, but out of respect and love for others. It's hard for me to believe that the forbidden isn't already there, since I evolve, like everyone else, in a space that is itself *a priori* normative. I can still see "the world as a game" (E. Fink), but this game has rules that I'm obliged to respect. The idea of my absolute freedom is something I live out in my imagination, to the rhythm of my inventions of another world, another society, other human relationships. By being already there, ambient normativity offers me a continuous representation of the rationality of my conduct, encouraging me to support and develop a basic existential rationalism, one that represents the equilibrium for the survival of human beings.

The temptation of the illicit takes a more subtle turn when it is inherent in the way each person tries to live his or her own madness. But it is the capacity of human beings to repress that remains the essential prerequisite for the mental integration of prohibitions. This is an almost natural predisposition to make prohibition the main cog in the wheel of guilt. Freud distinguishes between repression, which remains unconscious, and the judgment of condemnation, which appears above all in the course of treatment, when the patient consciously decides to keep away certain objects of impulse that he considers reprehensible. Condemnation would be a way of recognizing the necessity of prohibitions, whereas repression is merely a defense mechanism by which we endure them. Is it just a "realization" that legitimizes the role of the forbidden?

In short, by revealing the complex origins of our repression, the analytical treatment makes it possible for us to accept the judgment of condemnation as a conscious means of accepting the forbidden. In other words, the scenic constructions of the *little polymorphous pervert* we were as children are revised and corrected, so that after the treatment, we can assume respect for the forbidden in good understanding with ourselves. The ideal psychic equilibrium would then depend on lowering the level of guilt in our ways of living with prohibitions.

The obsessional lives in love and enjoyment of the forbidden, without feeling the slightest guilt. They "barricade themselves", you might say. Protection against the other always has an obsidional aspect. The obsessive protects himself by remaining on the alert, ready to spy on

anything that might be a threat. And, to this end, he will construct an entire surveillance apparatus, so that he himself becomes the object of his obsession without realizing it. In Kafka's short story *The Burrow*, the form given to the beast who is also the narrator remains difficult to grasp. As you read, the animal takes on the appearance of a human being, developing tactics to build and develop the place where he imagines himself protected from outside threats. It accumulates everything it needs to hold a siege, digging, tirelessly pursuing the construction of its hole in which, outside of time, it deliriums and goes mad. Such is the paradox presented by Kafka: man constructs the prison in which he imprisons himself. Obsessive neurosis and paranoia come together in this darkly humorous tableau. If the threats are self-generated, there's nothing to suggest a peaceful state, because the enemy is the other. According to Kafka's allegory, man is the victim of his own trap, and his tranquility can only be experienced through the threat of losing it. It is the other who is "forbidden".

3. Reading the Forbidden

THE PROHIBITION IS MOST OFTEN REPRESENTED BY A RED CIRCLE INTERSECTED BY A DIAGONAL LINE RUNNING THROUGH THE PROHIBITED OBJECT AND GESTURE. The proliferation of pictograms risks creating visual pollution in the same way as the proliferation of advertising posters. Their configuration is visible from a distance, even if the design of what is prohibited is not recognizable. The prohibition is thus announced before its object. When there is a set of pictograms, we remain rather perplexed, not to say "forbidden", even if a large sign announces that we are welcome. **Before we succeed in deciphering the prohibited gestures, a certain atmosphere of prohibition is imposed, most often for the protection of the environment.** We need to understand that the land we're about to enter is "precious" and that safeguarding its natural authenticity depends on our "good behavior". Indeed, the Conservatoire du Littoral has "frozen" some seaside landscapes to prevent any degradation. Even walking is forbidden. This is the price we have to pay to save the virginity of a nature controlled by man. We can dream of the beauty of what remains inaccessible to us, and consider it fortunate that natural purity no longer runs the risk of being soiled by man. In the Philippines, a territory inhabited by "primitive men" was thus off-limits to ethnologists from all over the world, in order to save the origin of this primitiveness. North Americans like to preserve this image of the virginity of a territory and its people, untouched by the effects of contemporary modernization.

The universality of the pictogram signifying prohibition is undeniable. Most often comprehensible in all languages, its semantic evidence guarantees absolute sovereignty. Uncertainty can only come from the design itself, from the representation of the prohibited gesture or object. **But the uncertainty of perception can be great, when we no longer know what we should or shouldn't do.** At the end of a street, for example, we come up against a wall on which one sign tells us that it's forbidden to turn right, and the other to turn left. It's not just a bad dream, it's a rare but plausible occurrence. This cancellation of the alternative by contradictory prohibitions provokes one of the most beautiful existential questions! What to do when there's no alternative?

The prohibition can be expressed by a sign with a text stating what not to do, or by a pictogram that is supposed to give us a representation of what is prohibited. There are hardly any signs prohibiting urination, which represent the impossibility of fulfilling this "natural" need. However, I discovered one in a book: the trajectory of urination is represented by a dotted line, crossed out by a red line. What about spitting? If the ban on spitting is no longer visible on walls or on public transport, is this a sign that "good habits" have been integrated? Are the "old" prohibitions destined to become part of humanity's intangible heritage?

Curiously, the ban imposed in other times seems to have been so well integrated that it makes it possible to forget it for a moment: I can spit in a metro corridor—which, we agree, is rude—and I won't get a fine, whereas if I light a cigarette, I'm likely to get one. In China, the habit of spitting on the ground is so pervasive that it is said that tourists must be happy in the evening when they realize that no salivary trace has soiled their shoes. During the 2008 Olympic Games, the Chinese government attempted to impose a ban on spitting in the street, which Beijingers relatively respected until the end of the international festivities. But has this collective tradition disappeared? The public sphere is made up of territories where constant confrontation prompts users to be vigilant in defending their "living space". In Japan, a sneeze

in a subway carriage is enough for people to move aside in indignation. Wearing a mask signifies that one's neighbor's breath is dangerous. **Fear of contamination leads to a sovereign need to protect the body.**

As we have seen, with SARS, wearing a hygiene mask, although an effective means of preventing the virus from circulating, meant that every individual became a potential danger. It was the circulating mass of individuals with masked mouths that itself maintained the representation of a daily haunting of contagion. The implementation of sanitary control measures against a grave danger resembles the rehearsal of a disaster simulation exercise. Fear itself takes on a viral form, and can spread in the same way as the virus. It's a social archetype: the behaviors adopted to ward off viral fear express this primitive belief in the reactivation of the self-preservation instinct. But the more visible these preventive measures become, the faster they increase the rate of expansion of collective anguish. Society—like a social body threatened from all sides—is forced to see itself as a mirror of its possible decomposition.

We understand why the phenomenon of contagion inspires science fiction: the vision of increasingly frightened everyday life imposes a futuristic projection of an eventual return to the savage state, which can only be stopped by the exacerbation of control. The sanitary management of an epidemic seems to be an ideal example of how the measures applied are "geopolitical" signs of civic behavior. For a nation, it's no longer a question of hiding the extent of the danger, but of maintaining the global media theater of the eradication of its causes. **And it is the body itself that becomes the bearer of the signs of the forbidden.**

AND DO ANIMALS ESCAPE SUCH A SANITARY ONSLAUGHT? We all know that dog poo on the sidewalk is increasingly prohibited. We'll never forget the motocrottes which, in the city of Paris, had a hard time erasing traces of canine defecation. Nowadays, signs indicating areas reserved for dogs and bags for collecting such natural waste can be spotted, in addition to the signs reserved for humans. "I love my neighbourhood, I pick it up". But does this multiplication of pictograms suggest that individuals only obey the codes of such urban semantics? Do we still need this "call to order"?

MANY OF THE BEHAVIORS WE PRACTICE AS CIVIL ETIQUETTE ARE BASED ON OUR UPBRINGING, and the codes we apply function on the basis of implicit bourgeois prohibitions: when I set the table, I must not place the fork to the right of the plate. The codes of bourgeois "good manners" oblige us to consider "what is not done" as a possible fault. These are obligations that do not involve politeness, which presupposes a relationship with others, a response to a situation. On a bus, even young people, even strangers, often give up their seats for me when they see my white hair and my apparent difficulty in walking. **Politeness makes us forget the atmosphere of a prescription always designated by signals.** It retains

a charm beyond propriety, as if it could surprise us with the attention that the polite gesture gives us. Because it retains a note of anachronism, a polite gesture becomes a sign of elegance when performed in the present moment. **To be elegant is to forget, with a certain grace, that our gestures are governed by prohibitions.**

CIVIC-MINDEDNESS COULD BE DEFINED AS A WAY OF RESPECTING RULES IN COMMON, sharing a certain decorum in social life. From now on, I'm obliged to be the "bearer of the forbidden", denouncing "loud and clear" those who don't respect the rules. No more elegance towards neighbors! If I don't denounce, I become an accomplice to an act of transgression committed by another. Because of the failure of polite gestures, will civic-mindedness in the future have to be the repetitive exercise of police gestures? There's no need for a uniform; I find myself obliged to "represent" the forbidden in the eyes of others when they don't respect the rules. The entire management of public spaces implies a constant incitement to increasingly conspicuous sharing of what is forbidden.

So it is with the demarcation of a private space. A teenager will put a "No Trespassing" sign on his bedroom door to make it clear that he's at home, and that he wants to keep what he's doing there a secret. Privacy is achieved through our belief in signals that indicate boundaries that must not be crossed. "Naughty dog" or "electronic surveillance": space considered private is a bastion. The expression "trespassing", excessive as it may seem, forces us to conceive of intrusion as an overbearing act. Erving Goffman speaks of the "territories of the ego", the most essential of which seems to be "personal space", that "portion of space which surrounds an individual and where any penetration is felt by him as an encroachment which provokes a manifestation of displeasure and sometimes withdrawal".[1]

1. GOFFMAN (Erving), *The Staging of Everyday Life. Tome II: Les Relations en public*, Paris, Éditions de Minuit, 1973, p. 44.

Every individual organizes his or her territorial protection in an implicit, unreflected way. A kind of demarcation whose final representation is the protection of intimacy. This territorial inscription of the ego is made visible by bodily attitudes in the public space, where our intimacy remains under threat. But self-protection cannot be dissociated from games of provocation and seduction, which always call for the violation of limits. The propriety of this "defensive position" becomes active only insofar as it is challenged, otherwise self-protection becomes an enclosure—which, of course, can happen when humor is lacking. If the privatization of space becomes obsessive, it is no longer the freedom to be oneself that is protected, but rather the hatred of the other that prevails.

But this doesn't mean that private space is a no-holds-barred territory. Far from it! In many homes, a smoke detector hangs from the ceiling in the living room, and an audible signal warns neighbors if a smoker has forgotten that "at home" the ban must be the same as in public places. And in the kitchen or bathroom, *eco-gestures* are de rigueur: sustainable development limits the use of towels, soaps, water and electricity… In the past, the obligation to turn off the light when leaving a room was summed up in an amusing phrase: "This isn't Versailles! Sumptuary spending was reserved only for the rich. Today, all *waste* is part of humanity's peril. And the word waste itself is no longer used. It's taken for granted that water flows in illuminated fountains all night long, while at home, people are careful to save water and electricity.

What's good for the planet; what's good for your health... Anything that's "good for" is no longer a problem; all you have to do is accept, once and for all, that recommendations are orders. Culinary diets introduce daily constraints that result in prohibitions invoked as if in a litany *of what-is-not-good-for-you*. But you'd have to be pretty naive to think that Coca-Cola is less harmful than wine. Food prohibitions seem to set the mood for an ever healthier life. They constitute a charter that governs behavior patterns in both private and public life. **This presupposes a surprising mental integration of the beneficial universality of the ban.** The circle is complete: food codes, however confused they may seem, are there to ward off the risk of viral contagion, like the signals of a cordon sanitaire encompassing the private and the public.

TO WHAT EXTENT HAS THE NEED TO BAN BECOME THE NEW DRIVING FORCE BEHIND SOCIAL COHESION? It blurs the boundaries between the private and public spheres. Our need to forbid is most often triggered by our desire to preserve the smallest shared part of our intimacy. The other is the one who violates my privacy. Is it not this mania for forbidding that stimulates a new form of social bonding when it lets us see the agonies produced by our loss of intimacy?

Contemporary exhibitionism, made possible by communication tools, ends up making us forget the pleasures of

restraint and secrecy. Is the pictogram prohibiting the use of cell phones on trains simply a reminder of the need for discretion? It's the commuters who take public space for granted, like congruent portions of their private space. And if someone approaches someone whose headphones are blaring to the point of grinding his or her teeth, just to let them know they're on the verge of a nervous breakdown, they're likely to hear a string of insults, since they're intruding on the "private" sound space of the techno music enthusiast. The compulsion to forbid bursts forth when everything is both "private" and "public".

4. Freedom by Default

IS THE FEELING OF FREEDOM EXPRESSED IN A WAR OF PROHIBITIONS? The confrontation, in the public space, of our ways of forbidding, producing social bonds, would lead us to believe in the salutary exercise of defending freedoms.

But how can the feeling of freedom be experienced through self-exposure? A star will say she feels free because she can do whatever she wants, because she's so successful. But what about a star who does nothing but be a star, like this young woman called Paris Hilton? Her whole life and all her activities are devoted to showing off, both for herself and for an audience that she strives to seduce with her presence, her mannerisms and her body movements. True, she has the power to be rich, thanks to the fortune of her father, the billionaire Hilton, but she is neither a singer nor a film actress. Her talent lies in fulfilling the daily life of a star, surrounded by the paparazzi she

needs to maintain her public image. The countless obligations that such a staging of oneself implies could lead one to believe that this star knows no freedom, that she is so emptied of herself that she no longer belongs to herself for a single moment. She devotes herself to a cult of exhibitionism that must never fail. Some journalists would say that she has become a pure object, and that in this sense, she is fulfilling Andy Warhol's prophecy that the fulfillment of the society of spectacle and consumerism is starization. "I want to be as famous as a can of Campbell's soup. What she plays out on the public stage is the paradox of a feeling of freedom that is experienced in its radical negation. **She invents her own necessity to display her freedom of being.** You can always say that she's got nothing on her mind, that she's a pure product of consumer society, but she constitutes herself a "golden prisoner of the system" to exalt her sense of freedom.

How can we make an apology for emancipation today[2]? Emancipation would be a naive attempt, to say the least, to believe that we can free ourselves from the power of the social models of our representations. Only our madness can offer us a way out, a way through. **To live one's madness is to play with the forbidden without feeling any real guilt.** This madness can be destructive for others when all representation of limits disappears, when its staging becomes demonic in its irreducible determination to make the other its object. Any madness experienced on a daily basis tends

2. Jacques Rancière.

to construct its own figures of what "makes law", resulting in the need to subjugate the other.

We know that incest is an abhorrent experience. But if a father and daughter love each other to the extent that they do not respect the prohibition of incest, their affair, most often kept secret, will cause the prohibition to be concealed, as if their love triumphed over the power attributed to ethical and social rules. Madness and love do not really lead to transgression of the forbidden, but keep it at bay, like *the memory of a limit*. Passion blinds limits.

The law functions as a "call to order", to put back on the "right path" those who have allowed themselves to be carried away by their madness. The invocation of this return to the memory of the limit serves as an appeal to common reason, which remains founded on respect for the prohibitions established to maintain the symbolic order of any society. As a condition for the recognition of objective rationality, prohibition is the foundation of the need for a common order defined by limits that must not be crossed.

But the limits that psychoanalysts attribute to madness are those of suffering. In Peter Brook's staging of Tourette's syndrome, the dialogues between patient and psychiatrist are punctuated by a silence that closes the exchange between the rational logic of one and that of the other. The

patient's coherence never fails; it only remains out of step with the psychiatrist's, but it comes to nothing, except at the moment when the discrepancy produces his suffering. The limit emerges not between the coherence of psychiatric discourse and the incoherence of madness, but with the obligatory recognition of a social non-place for the rationality of madness itself. And yet, this is the paradox in which we live: we all know that the organization of society is the mediatized narration of collective madness. As a result, our representation of limits seems to emerge against a backdrop where all forms of madness clash.

The symbolic order of society is based on prohibitions that limit the individual's impulsive activity and prevent him or her from "acting out". Hidden behind a bush in a public park, the exhibitionist will attempt to satisfy his fantasies by revealing his naked sex, while the voyeur will find a hiding place to satisfy his scopic impulse. Is the impossibility of complying with an interdiction merely a sign of pathology? Anyone who does the wrong thing, and can't seem to control his or her impulses, is branded mentally ill. Even if his "act" calls out to others, his condemnation remains final. **The symbolic order does not tolerate the slightest failure that could lead to its destruction.**

When the media reveal, like a news item, a sordid act carried out by an individual whom no one could have imagined could act in such a way, the surprise is not due to an unexpected change in behavior, it comes above all from a refusal to conceive of such a reversal. This individual would have given no indication of what he might one day turn out to be capable of. The other, the one who looks like us, the one we meet every day when shopping, the other we greet and respect, we suddenly learn from a newspaper that he has committed a monstrous crime, that he took part in a gang rape, that he ate his grandmother... Nothing had appeared

to us until now, nothing that could lead us to suspect such a horror. And yet, we're not so surprised. On reflection, we realize that he was already showing the signs of his ignominy.

Our suspicions are aroused in reverse, as if we had been deceived, while recognizing that certain clues to which we had not paid enough attention had nevertheless been given to us by his behavior, too discreet to be honest. But don't these clues come from our own unconscious, as if another of ourselves could be the perpetrator of such a crime?

IS ALL HUMAN BEHAVIOR SUSCEPTIBLE TO SUCH REVERSION? If, from the top of a rampart, a man photographs a naked girl on the beach, is he committing a real crime? We'll think he's a paedophile, that he's building up a private collection, that he'll use such photographs on an Internet site, which will be accessible to all paedophiles… We also can't ignore the fact that the current haunting of paedophilia makes many gestures and attitudes towards children equivocal. **Even tenderness becomes a threat because it expresses emotional ambivalence.** In the eyes of others, any individual can appear to hide a sexual perversion, since the double of himself is revealed by his complex relations with taboos. What is held as taboo provokes, as everyone experiences, a singular attraction that lets us imagine that our desires are constantly measured against what is prohibited.

When Freud refers to children as polymorphous perverts, he's implying that our sexual life is rooted in a versatility of impulsive predispositions that are the building blocks of our neurotic obsessions. In this sense, we unconsciously choose the prohibitions that distress us, but which we believe we can enjoy transgressing. The scenography of transgression, often repetitive and identical, is presented as a "rape of the forbidden". **Moralism then functions as a reminder of the rule that can prevent the "act" or condemn it when it has been carried out.** However, it is no longer ethical values that prevail, although they are invoked, but the mechanism of Puritan rigorism that turns the forbidden into a scarecrow. The impulsive tension produced by the "violation of the forbidden" becomes an irreducible threat to the moral order of society, and imposes itself as a figure of human monstrosity.

THE "VIOLATION OF THE FORBIDDEN", WHICH COULD PASS FOR A PRIVATE ACT THAT CONCERNS ONLY ONESELF, IS IMMEDIATELY PROJECTED INTO THE "PUBLIC SPHERE" because it most often reveals relations of domination between the sexes. Its scenography often implies a "negation" of the other, even if he or she consents, even if he or she derives pleasure from it. But it can, as many literary authors have shown us, lead to the pleasures of connivance, as it challenges the very founda-

tions of domination. It doesn't reveal the dysfunction of a society, but rather those who maintain its symbolic order. Aren't the Marquis de Sade's scenes a cruel parody of domination? When the desire to transgress the forbidden becomes an obsessive mechanism in sexual life, psychoanalysts speak of a return to the parental "primitive scene". Is this not also a reappearance of the "primitive scene" of society itself? A mise en abyme of what every society has had to conceal in order to display its own symbolic coherence against the savagery of impulses.

The ethical and ideological discourse provoked by the "violation of the forbidden", when everyone gives their opinion, expresses their indignation, forges the public scene of the disaster that the collapse of moral rules could produce. **The "underbelly" of society is suddenly revealed.** And democracy, so often abused, universally imposes its essential foundation: the same rules for all. No power protects those who commit a major offence, and no citizen can go unpunished.

A political leader has the right to send thousands of men into harm's way, but not the right to be above the law when he breaks the law. His sovereignty is not so absolute as to absolve him. But he becomes a hero in spite of himself by embodying the taboo. The theory of the scapegoat is not enough to explain how a society builds its cohesion. When the perpetrator is a public figure, he is not a victim, but takes full responsibility for the "violation of the forbidden". His ability to master any situation implies exemplary self-control, since his public function is precisely to control the unexpected. Business leaders have demonstrated such

leadership skills by taking major risks, such as throwing themselves off a bridge with a rubber band. Some time ago, Brazilian President Collor parachuted to the ground to prove that he was capable of assuming supreme power. It's more difficult to imagine that what we take for a sign of sexual pathology could be a challenge.

Determining the offence, the primary aim of legal drama, involves a complex procedure whose knowledge overrides the fluctuations of moral sentiments. But morality has nothing to do with the procedural spirit; it doesn't use guilt as the driving force behind judgement, and sees the "violation of the forbidden" as contempt for the values on which it is founded. The outrageous media coverage of the "violation of the forbidden" is like a gigantic cathartic scenography, thanks to which society, seizing the opportunity of a masterly "passage à l'acte", offers itself the collective illusion of its purification.

Each of us nurtures our own sense of freedom as a traditional source of enjoyment. In this way, we preserve the imaginary part of our independence from social determinism. And despite the unconscious application of society's coercive models, the challenge is always to imagine that we are free. Yet it's the violation of what's forbidden that "beats the measure", as if consent to obey rules and codes, like sleeping water, only conceals the irreducible desire to transgress the forbidden. The "passage à l'acte" can then only be taken as a pathological sign, because it distorts conventional representations of the feeling of freedom. We need to attribute an unconscious overdetermination to "acting out" in order to radically deny the liberation it represents. In short, we have to see that it fails, then depreciate it, in order to recognize that the energy invested in carrying it out is worthy of better use.

5. Censorship Virus

MANY PEOPLE ARE PROTESTING AGAINST AN EXCESS OF PERMISSIVENESS THAT WOULD JEOPARDIZE THE ORDER OF SOCIETY. Marriage between homosexuals has not been voted for by the Chamber of Deputies. A member of parliament is even reported to have said: "And why not marriage with animals?", without being prosecuted for having made "degrading remarks", whereas the law of December 30, 2004 punishes the authors of remarks provoking "hatred or violence" or "insult committed under the same conditions against a person or a group of persons because of their sex, sexual orientation or handicap".

There is a growing divide between those who want to maintain traditional values and those who are striving to change society. What some see as evolution is an unacceptable sign of regression for others. The most timid will say that "it's premature". Is permissiveness based on the lifting of taboos? Is a society's progress measured by the gradual disappearance of certain fundamental prohibitions?

What becomes permissible, and was not before, is presented as a victory for equal rights or, for those who are designated as reactionaries, as a manifest error that is leading

society to its ruin. **Permissiveness is not tolerance. It is achieved under the pressure of prohibitions or taboos to be overcome. It remains the object of a struggle.** This is the meaning of revolt against what is censored. The idealization of emancipation opens the doors of freedom to what is forbidden. But the lifting of certain prohibitions creates new ones, as if it were necessary to plug the gaps they create.

WHAT FORMS DOES CENSORSHIP TAKE TODAY? It's easy to delude oneself into thinking that censorship would have disappeared in a democracy that recognized all freedoms. Such a blunder is obvious when you consider how censorship is inherent in the codes that govern a society. It remains the essential mechanism for maintaining order, but above all, it is integrated into the human psyche, like an imaginary watchdog capable of suppressing any excess of freedom.

WHAT ABOUT THE INCREDIBLE POWER OF SELF-CENSORSHIP? **The apparent absence of censorship is not a sign of greater freedom, especially in the media; it's merely the deceptive effect of very active self-censorship.** Journalists obey the rules of censorship, which they are able to anticipate in order to avoid its coercive effects. They know "what not to say", and it is by knowing this that they can continue to believe in their freedom of expression. Since

censorship is frowned upon by public opinion, it is preferable not to exercise it ostensibly. The political powers, along with those of finance, control the language of "bien-pensant" without needing to intervene, self-censorship being practiced through hierarchical mechanisms that make it possible to limit the audacity of certain journalists.

All the information that circulates seems all the more conventional since the Internet has become the place for the transmission of information described as "rumors" that are not always reliable. The belief in a new form of freedom of expression is then granted to the Net, as if the press were bound hand and foot, while keeping a smile on the face of propriety. The prevailing idea is that, with the Net, we can increasingly push back the limits of censorship or transgress them, while the press and audiovisual media will be increasingly "muzzled".

IN A TOTALITARIAN STATE, CENSORSHIP REMAINS CONSPICUOUS, AND SPEECH AND WRITING ARE SUBJECT TO PERMANENT CONTROL THAT IS NOT EASY TO CIRCUMVENT. In Brazil, during the dictatorship, the famous singer Chico Buarque avoided prison thanks to the linguistic prowess of his songs. *Despite you, today you're in charge… Despite you, tomorrow will be another day*. These lyrics have been mistaken for those of a love song, when in fact the pronoun *toi* refers to the dictatorship itself. The inversion of meaning is so well hidden that it is no longer legible or audible, nor does it reveal any subversive intent. But language games have their limits when it comes to the practices of censors, who are always able to use torture to impose the meaning that satisfies the reasons for their accusation.

In the days of the "Eastern bloc", ideological control over the use of language was difficult to circumvent, and in Central Europe, it was necessary to invent ways of speaking that required the ability to resort to double-speak, masking any overly virulent critical expression. The best-known stylistic practice is that of eulogizing in order to vilify a mode of discourse or a person. **Humor remains an essential weapon for diverting ideological discourse.**

There are no pictograms for "language bans" yet, only "good" education obliges us not to use certain words that are too coarse. But in Turkey, the Telecommunication Communication Presidency recently decided to ban one hundred and thirty-eight words from the Internet, including *sister-in-law*, *animal*, *nude*, *girl* and English words such as *pic*, which in Turkish means "bastard", and *got*, which means "buttocks". This rule is forcing certain sites to close down, establishing censorship on an illegal basis, since information on the constitution of the list has not even been provided. **While the rules of grammar remain unchallenged in any language, the same cannot be said for words, whose unrestricted use guarantees our freedom of thought.** Censorship pictograms may appear one day, and we imagine forbidden words in a red circle, with a fatal bar cutting them in two.

We like to believe that censorship does not exist in a so-called liberal society. **The control of our freedoms does not seem to limit our desires, our intentions, our ways of being or speaking.** This gives us the illusion of an ironic marginality that is always possible, secures our belief in the "second-degree" use of language, and reinforces our illusion of being able to "distance ourselves" from the conventions of an overly "politically correct" meaning. The violent figure of the forbidden—the "*strinck verboten*" of the Nazi era—is part of our subterranean and ageing memories, and if we sometimes feel that we are living another contemporary form of totalitarianism, this one is so devious that it is able to make us believe in the still possible freedom of our aspirations. In France, the 1955 law on the state of emergency, passed at the time of the Algerian war, has not been repealed. It authorizes the Ministry of the Interior to take "any measure to ensure control of the press and radio". Cartoonists' drawings and phrases are sometimes censored. In 2007, cartoonist Placid was fined for writing this sentence about identity checks: "Facies checks, although prohibited by law, are not only commonplace, they are multiplying." But "a person who has been censured" no longer seems to be subject to harsher penalties.

HAS CENSORSHIP TAKEN ON OTHER, MORE INSIDIOUS FORMS? In our daily lives, the organization of the cultural market leads us to believe that everything is possible, and that our choices can follow the rhythm of an endless alternative. Yet there's a paradox here: when everything seems to be immediately possible, without our being able to feel any "becoming of the possible", it's our freedom of choice that takes on a constraining air.

If the possible is "already given", it no longer has any revelatory power. An artist may appear to be able to do whatever he likes, but his creative freedom remains subject to models of what has gone before, which he may not even be aware of. It is the repetition of these models that, over time, establishes a space of implicit normativity for artistic creation. The "déjà-vu", the "déjà-fait", impose limits on the belief that "anything is possible". No longer the fruit of a conquest or the effect of an accident of reality, of an incongruity, the possible appears as the evidence of the acquired. Nothing seems to stand in the way of artistic creation. The mass effects of artistic production and their perpetual visibility in the public arena represent the illusion of incredible freedom of expression. When "everything is possible", the absence of public recognition in no way prevents each unrecognized artist—or those who do not seek to be known—from constructing their own singularity and maintaining it with a certain complacency. **Creative freedom is based on the illusion of representation, which is never censored.**

AS EVERYONE MUST HAVE THE FREEDOM TO EXPRESS THEMSELVES, ANY EXCESS OF CRITICAL VIOLENCE IS IMPLICITLY FORBIDDEN. Getting angry about commonly shared ideas quickly becomes an expression of rudeness. It's an outrage

against democratic consensualism. Hitting one's opponent in a public debate is taken as a sign of weakness, a loss of composure, on the principle that a punch is not an argument. Yet fights between "great intellectuals", with no shortage of philosophical arguments, happened in other times. Despite the ostentatious cries of people revolted for this or that reason, everything seems "hushed". Aren't public demonstrations themselves becoming archaic *echolalia*? This obligatory politeness is legitimized not by the so-called "pensée unique", but by the fact that agreement or disagreement passes through the forks of the formal and empty principle of democracy. The buffoonery of a rather mawkish courtesy feeds on the contemporary softness of the adage *il est interdit d'interdire*—which translates into a belief in the irreducible freedom of expression.

To be recalcitrant, whether you like it or not, is to be considered contemptuous or temperamental. Such is the rule of propriety by which the consensual sharing of the manifestations of each person's freedom ensures its social legitimacy. Any opposition to what is commonly believed is seen as an expression of reproachable contempt for others. **Censorship comes from the diktat imposed by the most conventional ideas.** Anyone who gets carried away in a public debate is overstepping the mark, and his or her intemperance is not worthy of his or her wrath. The "Indignés" in Spain are content to state the object of their indignation, and their moderate anger bears no resemblance to the outbursts of the "Enragés" of '68. The simulacrum of politeness in contemporary democracy annihilates aggression by making it unhealthy. Censorship is self-evident; it no longer needs to be decided, but is carried out in the name of democracy. **Everyone has the right to speak, so that everyone ends up saying the same thing.**

What is "not to be said" publicly is merely a misplaced and contemptuous negation of the consensus that imposes itself as implicit censorship. For such is the paradox: how can an agreement of thought, shared by the majority, be reversed into the power of censorship? Strange censorship, it's true, since it is also presented as the very expression of a collective freedom shared by all. From now on, the whole purpose of language is to reproduce a conventional agreement capable of absorbing anything that opposes or resists it. It's easy to see why procedural hysteria has a future. **The inflation of legal procedures curiously increases the mania for prohibition.** There's the famous story of the American woman who was awarded a substantial compensation because, being pregnant, she had drunk a lot of whisky, which had damaged her pregnancy. The label did not say: "Whisky is forbidden to pregnant women". A prohibition that is not ostensibly signified makes legal proceedings possible. Will the essential function of language be to express the prohibition? And will the recalcitrant be condemned to being nothing more than litigants?

IMAGES CAN ALSO BE BANNED. The exhibition "Parisians under the Occupation" at the Bibliothèque Historique de la Ville de Paris was banned shortly after opening. It had not been made clear that photographer André Zucca was working for the French edition of *Signal*, the German army magazine. The images were in color, as André Zucca had received Agfacolor film from the Germans. The overriding impression given by the exhibition is one of a certain serenity, as there are hardly any German soldiers to be seen in the Paris neighborhoods where the photographs were taken. According to Éric Hazan[3] , "this is the real scandal of this exhibition: it shows the difference between two parts of the city, the collaborationist part and the other".

Censorship came only after certain newspapers had expressed their indignation. What sense could it have made? No doubt the ambiguity should have been cleared up beforehand, by specifying exactly the context in which such photographs were taken. Revealing a "happy Paris" under the Occupation is an affront to the dignity of resistance fighters. Is it possible to be tricked into seeing images of elegant women alongside young men in verdigris uniforms at La Madeleine? Yet there's no doubt that this "Paris" was

3. HAZAN (Éric), *Paris sous tension*, Paris, La Fabrique, 2011, pp. 93-94.

protected by the spirit of the Collaboration. Is it necessary to show ignominy by signifying it? **Whatever the use of censorship, what is forbidden is the emergence of any ambivalence.** Even if we believe it is rightly applied against anything that scorns the memory of those who sacrificed themselves, it introduces the demarcation line of what produces the *bien-pensant.*

For any photograph taken in the street or on a beach, if you intend to distribute it, you have to ask people for permission, in the name of respect for privacy. However, the "right to an image" is claimed in the name of a truth that must not be concealed. It calls for the free circulation of images.

It's true that we live in an age of "image hysteria", and that in this context, a photographic image of any person, when taken in the public space, can be considered an invasion of privacy and, as such, provoke legal action. Images of places and monuments do not include those of people "standing there". Yet in a society where the mass of images is immeasurable, where the circulation of images is becoming increasingly uncontrollable, and where, above all, the right to one's own image is becoming a universal demand, it's hard to imagine that we can refer to a very specific legal framework for the use of images. Whether it's a violation of a "habeas corpus" or an abuse of appropriation, the act of photographing itself can be taken, the moment reality is captured "in real time", as a "flagrant misdemeanor". Cell phones make it possible to take countless photographs or video sequences in any situation and at a moment's notice. This seizure of the real is done with impunity, as if it were natural to photograph, on impulse, whatever happens, not even to our gaze, since this kind of repetitive act is accomplished, so to speak, before we see. This visual capture precedes the intention to look and cancels it out in a compulsion for immediate visualization.

The photographic image, whether taken with the intention of providing evidence, or without any specific intention, is a formidable means of denunciation. Its most common use resembles the practice of "video surveillance". Those who do not obey the rules of survival can be photographed in "flagrante delicto". And if it's the judiciary that mediates in the non-application of prohibitions, it's easy to see why censorship loses its police-like appearance, thanks to the jurisprudence generated by the use of images as evidence.

The violence of generalized censorship is no longer frontal, as in a totalitarian system; it is viral. It spreads without giving the impression of imposing any form of domination. It is based on unrestrained consent to the rules of survival, like the virus (or antivirus) that saves the community from destruction.

6. Ban Everything?

The triumph of consensualism, a devious form of censorship, puts us in a state of anticipatory acceptance of all forms of control, as if the inflation of normative decisions had become a sign of "good health" for the future. **The mania for prohibition is stimulated by consensus itself.** Containing the common part of our aggressiveness, it still expresses the illusion of a possible violence against resignation, whereas it is the weapon of our submission to consensus. **The adage *il est interdit d'interdire* no longer applies to the prohibition itself, but becomes the backdrop for consensualism, taking the place of our belief in freedom.** This is how we maintain the idea of being free when we are beset by the prohibitions imposed by the "right-thinking".

Some may recall this legendary scene: a man in the crowd exclaims "Mort aux cons!" ("Death to jerks!"), to which de

Gaulle replies, "Vaste programme!" ("Vast program!"). Such an outspoken statement may not have been intended for him, but the humorous elegance with which the General retorted without the slightest hesitation aroused admiration, far beyond political judgments on any side. No expression of contempt, just a masterly, ironic reversal of an exclamation that might have seemed hurtful.

Today, this finesse of wit is no longer appropriate. "Casse-toi, pauvre con", a now-famous interjection, betrays how contempt ignores humor. The atmosphere of consensual exchanges encourages us to rediscover the "primitive" path of a return to obscene brutality when we're angry. The "soft" consensus that is everywhere present, insofar as "agreement must always be found", is far more sovereign in its violence than the slightest desire for negation expressed in public. This authoritarian principle of mutual understanding forces us to reject any desire for opposition that we may nevertheless have. What's worse is that humor—which at least introduces the appearance of a game of limits—is itself banned when it risks becoming an uncontrollable detour of meaning. The limpness of indignation is pathetic, the "outburst" remains without echo, because meaning is reversible, as if "for" and "against" were the two ends of a weathervane that turns in all directions. Is it the irony of what's happening in the real world, the irony of "the situation", that will save us from the consensus of *bien-pensance*?

"The only question now, the right question, is *whether it's still possible not to ban everything absolutely*."[4] This would be the eternal reign of the "bien-pensant". Any individual freedom is considered harmful by the community, which survives on the obsessive need to multiply laws. The collective enjoyment of all prohibitions is akin to the assumption of protection. But if all prohibitions have been laid down, if there are no more prohibitions to conquer, we are left with the enjoyment of denunciation. We'll have to spend our time denouncing anyone whose overly individual behavior is an archaic sign of transgression. Collective happiness is sustained by the need to represent the forbidden as the only effective means of warding off the multiple threats to our daily lives.

Forbidding everything also becomes the best way to preserve the propriety of a community-wide freedom. A kind of *average freedom*. It wouldn't bother other people, because it would be the same for everyone. A freedom against which no one has anything to say or object. **A freedom that doesn't**

4. MURAY (Philippe), *L'Empire du bien*, Paris, Les Belles Lettres, 2010, p. 72.

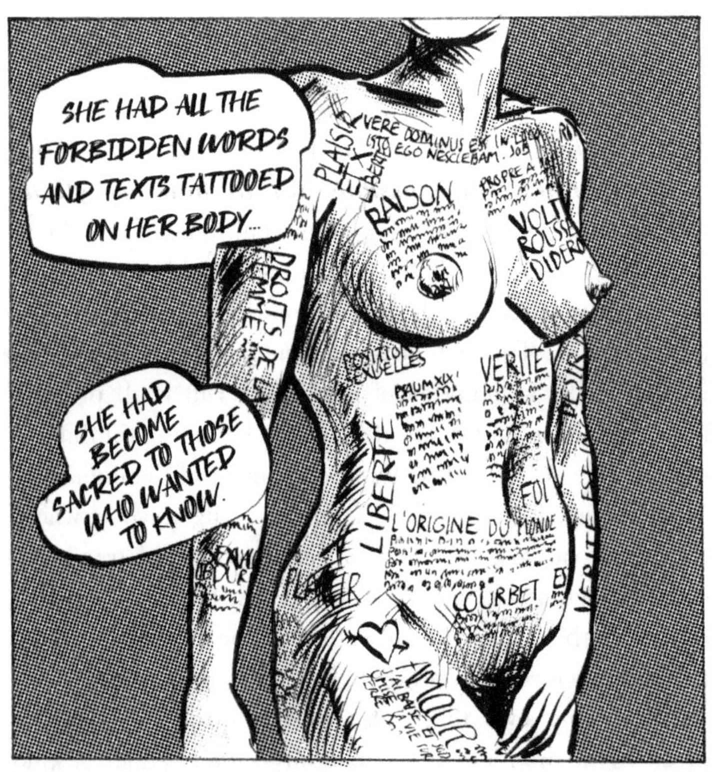

need to be publicly displayed, since its meaning would blossom within the constellation of prohibitions.

THE CONDITION OF THIS *AVERAGE FREEDOM* IS *PROHIBITION*. Prohibit in order to produce a social bond, to impose recognition of the social bond through a single mode of behavior that suits everyone. To follow to the letter the rules that are made for our collective survival, by denouncing those who are dangerous, all those "at-risk individuals" who lead us to suicide. Such a collective dynamic offers meaning to life. Prohibiting on a daily basis requires energy, and catalyzes that energy by giving it an objective purpose. It's a single, relentless struggle against everything that's bad for survival. Generalized prohibition is the eternal guarantee of all the virtues of the "bien-pensant".

SUBSTITUTING ITSELF FOR THE VALUES OF SOCIETY, THE FORBIDDEN ITSELF TAKES THE PLACE OF THE SUPREME VALUE. It may remain implicit, it may not need to be stated to be active, but it imposes itself as the raison d'être that protects our lives from the evils of excessive freedom. It is an irrefutable necessity for the future coherence of a global community governed by the same rules of survival. It is a weapon for repairing past errors and projecting a sustainable future. **And the death of free will completes voluntary collective servitude. The arbitrariness of norms is overcome by the proliferation of prohibitions.**

Good-natured skepticism is still allowed to suggest that the multiplication of prohibitions needs to be legitimized. But the legitimacy of prohibition is merely the trompe-l'œil of a coercive rationality with its cohort of "must haves". Not only is it "necessary" to comply with the norms of survival, but above all "necessary" to do so like everyone else. The benefits of voluntary obedience to the rules of mass survival should make all particularities of human behavior disappear. What some sociologists have called "mass individualism" is no more than a decadent figure of individuality. The expression of individual freedom, when reduced to the mere individualism of behavior, manifests itself as the chimera of an anachronistic "quant-à-soi". We no longer have any regard for the imaginative power of individuality. What is likely to produce singularity in our behavior is translated into a "depersonalized meaning belonging to all and to none"[5]. These are no more than the remnants of a singularity trapped in mass models. Provoking the repression of the imaginary, conformism relies on the reassuring repetition of the identical as the sole principle of adaptation.

5. SAMI-ALI (Mahmoud), *Le Banal*, Paris, Gallimard, 1980, p. 26.

Table of Contents

www.ingramcontent.com/pod-product-compliance
Lightning Source LLC
LaVergne TN
LVHW050324160826
845677LV00014B/3533

* 9 7 8 2 3 1 5 0 1 3 6 8 5 *